SAN XAVIER

The Spirit Endures

TEXT BY KATHLEEN WALKER

PHOTOGRAPHS BY *ARIZONA HIGHWAYS* CONTRIBUTORS

ARIZONA
HIGHWAYS

(ABOVE) *A dusting of snow accentuates the winter scene at Mission San Xavier del Bac.* (PREVIOUS PAGE) *These statues in the mission's interior depict, from left, St. Anthony of Padua, a popular Franciscan preacher and healer, holding the infant Jesus; a cherub amid decorative and symbolic flourishes on the altar; and the angel overlooking one corner of the east transept. Above the angel is a portion of the Franciscan cord used in the interior design scheme.*

CONTENTS

ABOUT THE AUTHOR

A frequent contributor to *Arizona Highways* on topics dealing with people and events in contemporary and historic Arizona, Kathleen Walker's interest in writing most often turns to the history and culture of Mexico, examining the impact they have had on today's Arizona. She received a bachelor's degree from the Universidad de las Americas in Mexico City and a graduate degree from Fairfield University, a Jesuit college in Connecticut. As a television reporter she covered events in Arizona and New Mexico. She now works as a freelance writer.

ACKNOWLEDGMENTS

The author and editors extend special acknowledgment to individuals and organizations whose cooperation and assistance were invaluable in producing this book. They include: Dr. Bernard Fontana, an anthropologist who has devoted much of his career to the study of San Xavier and other Kino missions; the Rev. Charles Polzer, S.J., curator of ethnohistory at the Arizona State Museum; the Arizona Historical Society in Tucson; the Center for Creative Photography at the University of Arizona; and Schneider Optics for providing state-of-the-art wide-angle lenses.

PHOTO CREDITS

JACK DYKINGA — front and back covers, pages 8, 9, 13, 16 (both), 17, 23, 24, 26 (bottom), 27, 28, 30, 31, 32-33, 38-39, 40, 41, 42, 50-51, 60-61, 65, 70, and 80.

RICHARD MAACK — back inside cover flap, pages 1 (all), 6, 7, 12, 22, 26 (top), 29, 36, 46, 52, 58, 68, 75, and 78 (top).

RANDY PRENTICE — front inside cover flap, pages 2, 18-19, 37, 48, 54-55, 62 (all), 69, and 79.

DON STEVENSON — pages 25 (both), 49, 53, 59, 63, 64, and 74.

BUEHMAN STUDIO — pages 44, 45, 56, and 57.

ANSEL ADAMS — pages 47, 67, and 71.
©The Ansel Adams Publishing Rights Trust, Collection of the Center for Creative Photography, The University of Arizona.

JOHN P. SCHAEFER — pages 20, 21, and 73.
©1977 John P. Schaefer, Collection of the Center for Creative Photography, The University of Arizona.

DICK ARENTZ — pages 76 and 77.
©1991 Dick Arentz, Collection of the Center for Creative Photography, The University of Arizona.

WILLARD CLAY — pages 43 and 72.

ESTHER HENDERSON — page 35.

TIMOTHY H. O'SULLIVAN — page 10.

CARLETON E. WATKINS — page 11.

XAVIER GALLEGOS/*TUCSON CITIZEN* — page 78 (bottom).

ILLUSTRATIONS

KATERI WEISS — pages 5 and 14-15.

BOOK EDITOR: BOB ALBANO
COPY EDITORS: BONNIE TRENGA AND EVELYN HOWELL
DESIGN: MARY WINKELMAN VELGOS
PHOTOGRAPHY EDITOR: RICHARD MAACK
RESEARCH EDITOR: STUART ROSEBROOK
PRODUCTION: ELLEN STRAINE

Prepared by the Book Division of *Arizona Highways*® magazine, a monthly publication of the Arizona Department of Transportation
PUBLISHER: NINA M. LA FRANCE
MANAGING EDITOR: BOB ALBANO
ART DIRECTOR: MARY WINKELMAN VELGOS
PRODUCTION DIRECTOR: CINDY MACKEY
PHOTOGRAPHY DIRECTOR: PETER ENSENBERGER

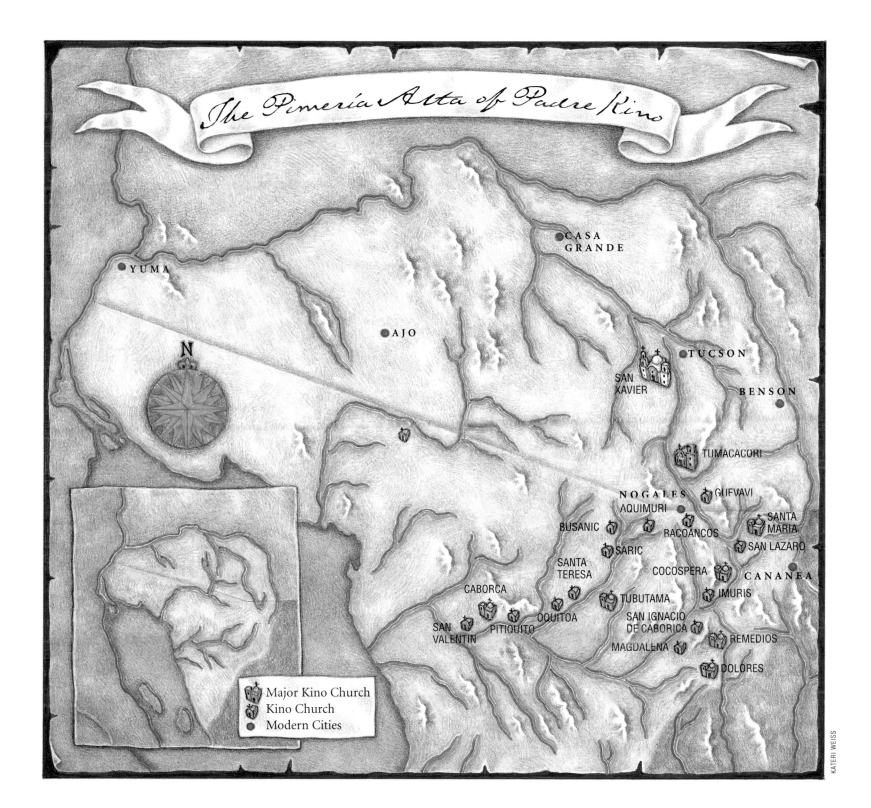

The Pimería Alta of Padre Kino

CASA GRANDE

YUMA

AJO

N

TUCSON

SAN XAVIER

BENSON

TUMACACORI

NOGALES
AQUIMURI
BUSANIC
BACOANCOS
SARIC
SANTA TERESA
CABORCA
OQUITOA
TUBUTAMA
SAN VALENTIN
PITIQUITO
SAN IGNACIO DE CABORICA
MAGDALENA

GUEVAVI

SANTA MARIA
SAN LAZARO
COCOSPERA
CANANEA
IMURIS
REMEDIOS
DOLORES

Major Kino Church
Kino Church
Modern Cities

KATERI WEISS

RICHARD MAACK

First Light

The photographers are the first to arrive at the old church.

They come with the dawn, hoping the light of this sunrise will add a glow to the elegant walls and the towers of the mission. They are here for the simple visions — a girl walking down the road wearing the dark uniform of her mission school, or a dog confidently making his own journey through the ancient land of the Tohono O'odham.

One photographer sets up equipment in the courtyard near the church's massive wooden doors. Another walks around the site, searching for an intriguing angle. A third, carrying a tripod, wanders onto the cactus-covered land around the structure.

Other photographers will wait for a special moment, perhaps on another day, when they believe the light to be perfect. Some have it down to a few minutes a year when the light can caress the almost-pink facade in such a way that makes you wonder if the builders knew it would be so.

The faithful come next. An older woman, dependent on the supporting arm of her younger companion, moves slowly toward the church. A cowboy approaches, wearing a white shirt fully buttoned to the cuffs. He walks in boots with the underslung heel of men who work the land of the Mexican state of Sonora. As it is for the women, this is his church. His family may have come to it for a hundred years or more to ask favors of the saints, to light the candles, to leave their prayers and hopes at its altars.

Inside the church, warmth replaces the last chill of the desert night. Candles lit the day before still are burning. Later, when the sun is high, the church will seem cooler than the desert beyond its doors. With walls up to six feet thick, the building can make its own temperatures.

The church, which has been compared to the Vatican's Sistine Chapel, is called the finest example of Spanish colonial architecture in the United States. But, many of the visitors who come here are not prepared for what they see. They pause in the doorway, stunned. One declares simply, "Oh, my," as she beholds the glory of the 18th century, the color, the joy, the passion, and the whimsy. "A fabulous thing," another will sigh.

Sounds of workers filter down from the roof. They belong to

(ABOVE) *Cherubs play a decorative and symbolic role at the mission. They are seen as casting light on spiritual themes.*
(RIGHT) *Considered the finest example of Spanish colonial art and architecture in the United States, the mission church of San Xavier del Bac inspires the faithful, enthralls the curious, and challenges artists.*

Sonny Morales' crew. Five generations of the Morales family

(ABOVE) *The woman in the radiant blue dress is one of the mission's three sculptures of Mary. Here she is* La Dolorosa, *or the Sorrowing Mother.*
(RIGHT) *San Xavier once marked the edge of the Spanish Empire, a welcome beacon to those few travelers across a lonely land.*

have worked on this church. "My church," says Sonny Morales.

Soon, skilled artisans will resume their work inside to preserve the artwork created when this church was an outpost of the Spanish Empire, a white beacon marking the edge of the Christian world.

A Franciscan priest crosses in front of the altar, dusty tennis shoes poking out from under his brown robe. He cleans away the used candles, making way for new ones. He moves quickly, but you can still see the patches on his robe. Above him a choir of angels sings.

The tour buses start arriving by 9 A.M. Making their first stop on a journey through the area south of Tucson, tourists spill out with cameras and straw hats. The parking lot is filling with cars and RVs, one as big as a hotel suite.

Local trucks and cars are passing the front of the church. Men at the steering wheels tip their hats; women make the sign of the cross. They may have passed this church twice a day, five days a week, year after year, but still they turn for another look.

This is the mission church of San Xavier del Bac, two centuries old, a place of faith and history. It has stood within the borders of three countries and withstood raids, abandonment, the destruction of time and nature, and the carelessness of humanity.

Standing before the mission now, a visitor raises his arms and says in wonder, "Right in the middle of nowhere!" Inside, an elderly man bends down to a young boy and whispers kindly, "Take off your hat." The boy does so without question. The builders of San Xavier del Bac knew it would be so.

FIRST LIGHT

The Foundations

TIMOTHY H. O'SULLIVAN, NATIONAL ARCHIVES AND RECORDS ADMINISTRATION.

The first known photograph of San Xavier (right) was taken in 1871 by Timothy H. O'Sullivan. A decade later, Carleton E. Watkins was among the first to photograph the mission and its surrounding landscape (far right) from the hill east of the church.

O'Sullivan's work shows his documentary style. At the time he photographed the mission, he was a member of the Wheeler Survey, one of the four major teams commissioned by the United States Government after the Civil War to produce detailed, illustrated reports on the West. Earlier, O'Sullivan worked with Matthew Brady in documenting the Civil War and on another Western survey.

Watkins' image of San Xavier — showing how the White Dove stands as a beacon in the desert — reflects his focus on landscape photography. His photographic work dates to the 1860s, when he stunned his contemporaries with his images of the Yosemite area.

RICHARD MAACK

CHAPTER ONE

The Foundations

FATHER KINO AND HIS HOLY CHAIN

The church of San Xavier del Bac dominates the desert nine miles south of Tucson, Arizona, and sits on 14 acres deeded to the Roman Catholic diocese of that city from an original grant signed in 1910 by President William Taft. The land surrounding the mission is part of the 2.84-million-acre Papago Indian Reservation, the land of the Tohono O'odham, the Desert People.

Set deep in the ground, the walls of the church are made of the land itself, clay fired to brick. At their core is volcanic rock. The plaster covering the structure dries white in the sun, earning the church the nickname "White Dove of the Desert."

The church was completed in 1797 under the leadership of the men of the Order of Friars Minor, Franciscans. But the name most associated with San Xavier del Bac is that of Father Eusebio Francisco Kino, a missionary who wore the black robe of the Society of Jesus, the

Jesuits. He was as tough as the land he rode in the late 1600s and early 1700s. He didn't build this church, but he did build many others, a chain of missions in what now is northern Sonora, Mexico, and southern Arizona.

San Xavier was to be but one link marking the long reach of the Christian World.

This wasn't his chosen land, the north of New Spain. Born in the Italian Tyrol, a region of the Alps, and educated in the Jesuit colleges of Europe, Kino had requested China for his missionary work. But with the vows comes obedience.

He was sent to New Spain and ultimately to the land called the Pimería Alta, a Spanish phrase meaning the land of the upper Pimas. Here he would live for 24 years and here he would die.

Bordered on the west by the Sea of Cortés, the Pimería Alta stretched north across what are now the Mexican state of

Sonora and southern Arizona. Mountain ranges and rivers cut the land, fertile valleys fed it, and the desert starved it. The hilltops offered ideal sites for mission churches. People atop them could look down at any who approached. Those below could look up at the structure, perhaps in awe.

The villages offered souls for the Faith. Tens of thousands of native people — Seris, Opatas, Pimas, and Apaches — lived in the 50,000 square miles of the Pimería Alta. These tribes would make themselves

(ABOVE) *With symbolism in mind, artists often assigned angels the role of holding back drapery, as if they were opening the way for someone.*
(RIGHT) *The walls of today's San Xavier rose under the direction of the Franciscans in the late 1700s, but historic foundations are found in the work of Father Eusebio Kino, a Jesuit priest and explorer.*

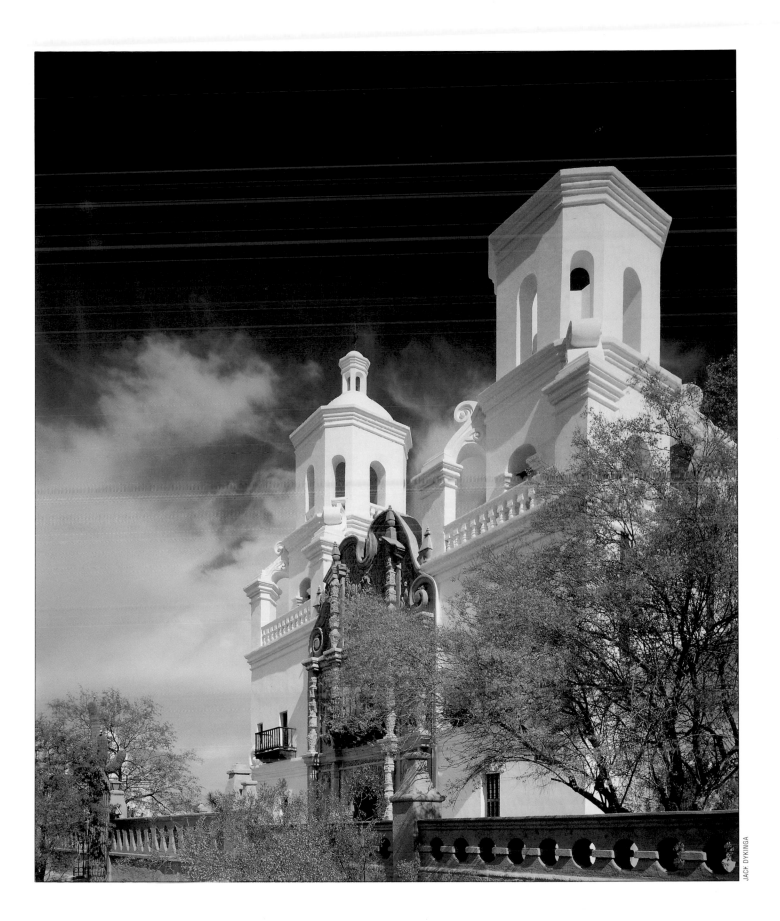

1687
The Jesuit priest Eusebio Francisco Kino arrives in the Pimería Alta.

1692
Father Kino first visits the O'odham village of Wa:k, christened San Xavier del Bac.

1700
Father Kino begins building a church at Wa:k.

1702
Father Kino makes his final visit to the mission.

WORLD EVENTS

1687	1700	1701	1715	1719
Sir Isaac Newton publishes Law of Universal Gravitation.	250,000 settlers live in North American colonies.	Yale College founded.	Christian missionaries banned in China.	Daniel Defoe publishes *Robinson Crusoe*.

1768
The Franciscans are given control of San Xavier del Bac and the other Kino missions. Father Francisco Hermenegildo Garcés is assigned to the mission.

1783
Construction of the present San Xavier del Bac church is believed to have begun.

1797
San Xavier del Bac is completed.

1827
Franciscans and others born in Spain are expelled from the newly independent Mexico.

WORLD EVENTS

1789	1796	1797	1822	1836
Mutiny on the H.M.S. Bounty.	Vaccination against smallpox introduced.	John Adams is 2nd president of U.S.	Early experimental photographic image made.	Alamo falls to Mexican troops.

1900
Bishop Henry Granjon begins major building project at the mission.

1910
President William Taft gives deed to 14 acres on which mission complex stands to the Catholic Church.

1913
The Franciscans return to San Xavier del Bac after 76 years.

1953
Cast iron replicas of the original pilasters are installed.

WORLD EVENTS

1891	1904	1910	1912	1950
The Adventures of Sherlock Holmes published.	Frank Lloyd Wright builds his first office building in Buffalo, New York.	Mexican Revolution begins.	Arizona becomes a state.	1.5 million television sets in U.S.

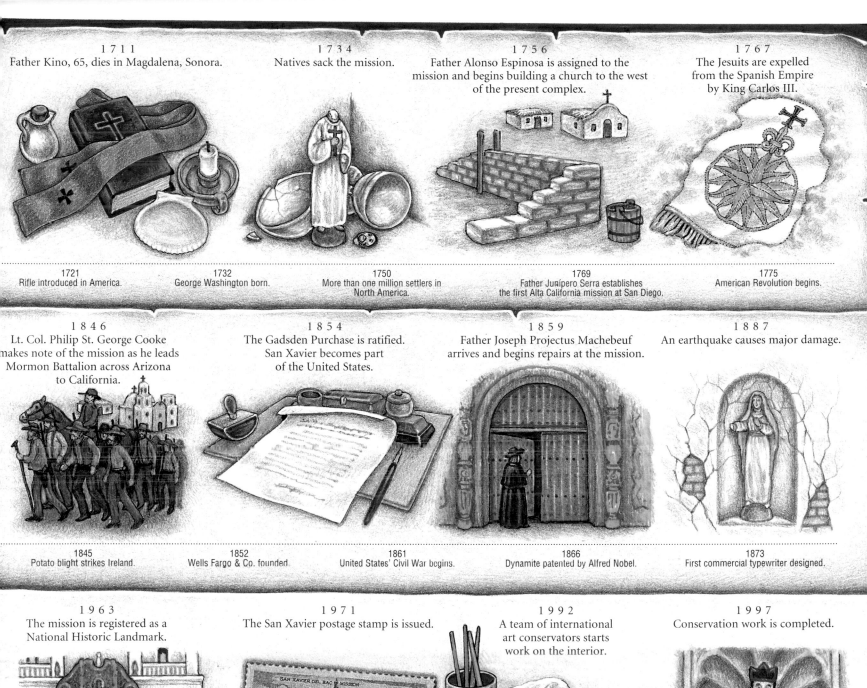

1711
Father Kino, 65, dies in Magdalena, Sonora.

1734
Natives sack the mission.

1756
Father Alonso Espinosa is assigned to the mission and begins building a church to the west of the present complex.

1767
The Jesuits are expelled from the Spanish Empire by King Carlos III.

1721
Rifle introduced in America.

1732
George Washington born.

1750
More than one million settlers in North America.

1769
Father Junípero Serra establishes the first Alta California mission at San Diego.

1775
American Revolution begins.

1846
Lt. Col. Philip St. George Cooke makes note of the mission as he leads Mormon Battalion across Arizona to California.

1854
The Gadsden Purchase is ratified. San Xavier becomes part of the United States.

1859
Father Joseph Projectus Machebeuf arrives and begins repairs at the mission.

1887
An earthquake causes major damage.

1845
Potato blight strikes Ireland.

1852
Wells Fargo & Co. founded.

1861
United States' Civil War begins.

1866
Dynamite patented by Alfred Nobel.

1873
First commercial typewriter designed.

1963
The mission is registered as a National Historic Landmark.

1971
The San Xavier postage stamp is issued.

1992
A team of international art conservators starts work on the interior.

1997
Conservation work is completed.

1963
President John F. Kennedy assassinated.

1968
The Rev. Martin Luther King Jr. and Sen. Robert F. Kennedy assassinated.

1972
Pocket calculators introduced.

1986
Challenger space shuttle explodes, killing seven crew members.

1997
Mother Teresa dies at age 88 in India.

JACK DYKINGA

well known to the people of the Kino missions.

Kino's travels put him in the saddle for an estimated 20,000 miles. When he slept, it is said, he used his saddle for a pillow. In his 50s, he could and did average 25 miles or more a day making the circuit of his missions and pushing the border of

(ABOVE) *The Franciscan churches of San Ignacio de Cabórica* (LEFT) *and San Diego de Pitiquito* (RIGHT) *stand along the Kino mission chain and still serve the people of Sonora.* (OPPOSITE PAGE) *In southern Arizona the mission of Tumacácori, another link in the chain, is now a national historical park and museum.*

the Spanish Empire ever north and west.

He would cross the uncharted land of the Tohono O'odham; be the first European to see the ruins of Casa Grande; travel up the San Pedro River and north to the Gila River; and search for proof that California was part of the mainland, not an island as most believed. He would also name a village in the Santa Cruz Valley San Cosme de Tucson.

Kino arrived in the Pimería Alta on March 13, 1687, and began his travels. On March 14, he stopped at the village of Cabórica and christened it San Ignacio. Within one month, building and planting had begun. This missionary work occurred 82 years before Father Junípero Serra would start

the first of his missions in California at a place christened San Diego.

The sites where Kino's missions rose, and the churches built after his death, still carry the names that mingled the language of the ancient people of the land with that of the new: San Diego de Pitiquito, San José de Imuris, San Antonio Paduano de Oquitoa, and Tubutama with its church named for San Pedro y San Pablo, St. Peter and St. Paul.

The mission chain included Dolores, Kino's home mission, now gone; Cocóspera, now in ruins but still hugging its hilltop; and Caborca, home of his fellow Jesuit and friend, Father Saeta. Saeta was killed, shot full of arrows during the 1695

uprising of those who chose not to follow the new religion and its priests. Shortly before his death he wrote to Kino, "Dear Father, don't lose sight of me."

Kino first visited Guevavi in 1691. Within a decade, Guevavi became the site of the first building erected by Europeans in southern Arizona. Now only melting adobe walls stand at what was once a *cabecera*, the term for a head mission. A few miles north was a *visita*, a smaller station, at Tumacácori. Now a national historical park, it remains a striking reminder of the mission era.

Still farther north, there was the large village of Wa:k, translated as "the place where the water emerges." Kino stopped

JACK DYKINGA

there in 1692 to speak to the 800 inhabitants. He named the village San Xavier del Bac in honor of St. Francis Xavier, one of the first Jesuits. He had died in 1552 on a mission to China.

To the people of the Pimería Alta, Kino brought both the Word and food. He introduced wheat and other crops. At the missions, fruit trees were planted, grapes grown, and livestock raised, beginning the cattle-ranching industry of today's Arizona and Sonora. He was running herds along his mission chain, not a few hundred head, but thousands.

"I ordered rounded up the 1,400 odd cattle which were here," he wrote at Dolores of his work in May 1700, "… and told the overseer that dividing them into two equal parts, he should take, as he did, one part to San Francisco Xavier del Bac …"

The missions became communities and supply stations serving miners and settlers.

At some of the missions Kino established, traces of the gardens still exist and fields are still farmed near them. But, of the original missions he built, nothing is left but names and sites. Later, missionaries built churches atop or near the original mission sites. Some of the Kino missions dissolved back into the earth that had given them birth and form. But today, the people of northern Sonora live, worship, and work where Kino once built. And they dance, sometimes, in the streets on the days set aside to honor those saints the Jesuit brought to the edge of the world.

Kino died at age 65 in 1711 at the mission of Santa María Magdalena. His burial place would remain undiscovered until 1966, when archaeologists found bones believed to be his and those of two fellow Jesuits. The skeleton is now on display in a glass-domed enclosure in a ramada-like structure adjacent to the church in Magdalena.

He had once asked to be allowed to move to San Xavier del Bac, but no replacement came for him at Dolores. So, he remained a visitor to Bac and started building a church there in April, 1700. He noted in his journal, "We began the foundations of a very large and capacious church and house of San Xavier del Bac, all the many people working with much pleasure and zeal." There is no evidence showing the exact location of the structure nor if it was completed.

The next church would be built by another Jesuit, Father Alonso Espinosa, in the 1750s. The location of that structure, which no longer exists, was just west of the present church.

The Franciscans would come to San Xavier del Bac after the Jesuits left. They would build where a tough man in a black robe had once stopped to speak of religion to the people.

"They listened with pleasure to these and other talks concerning God, heaven, and hell," Kino wrote, "and told me that they wished to be Christians and gave me some infants to baptize."

Kino showed them a map of the world and then changed theirs forever.

THE FRANCISCANS REPLACE THE JESUITS

Construction of today's church of San Xavier del Bac began around 1783 with a building fund of 7,000 pesos. The money was borrowed against a yet-to-be-planted wheat crop. The next 14 years of work were directed by men who then wore robes of undyed wool cinched with rope. These followers of the gentle path of St. Francis of Assisi replaced the Jesuits at the missions of the Pimería Alta.

King Carlos III expelled the Jesuits from the Spanish Empire in 1767. He was following the lead of other European rulers in eliminating the "black-robes" from positions of power. The rulers believed the Jesuits had misused power at every level. In the Pimería Alta, the Jesuits who came after Kino had continued protecting the native people from becoming a labor force for the Spanish mines and ranches. Others would say the Jesuits were keeping native labor for their own use at the missions. And, under the Jesuits, the native converts of the mission system were not becoming much-needed tax-paying citizens of the crown.

So, the Jesuits were marched out of the missions and the Franciscans were ordered in. They knew the way. They had been there before, among the very first.

In 1539, the Franciscan Fray Marcos de Niza entered the Pimería Alta with a scout named Esteban, a Moor who had been a slave. Among the goals of the de Niza expedition was to find the fabled Seven Cities of Gold in a land called Cíbola. Esteban forged ahead of the priest and went north across Arizona and to his death in Zuniland in northwestern New Mexico. De Niza followed Esteban's trail, set a cross upon a hill near the less-than-golden pueblos of the Zuni, then returned to Mexico City. His trek covered 2,000 miles. He walked.

De Niza would travel north again on part of the Coronado expedition of 1540. On this expedition, one of the true treasures of the land was seen by Europeans for the first

(ABOVE) *The ancestral land of the O'odham surrounds San Xavier, which still presents a vision of a world untouched by modern life.*

time, the Grand Canyon.

Franciscan missionaries had served in Sonora with the Jesuits during the early years of colonization, but in 1652 were ordered to stay in the lands east and north of the Pimería Alta. They built missions in what is now New Mexico, Texas, and northern Arizona. But by 1768, they were back in the Pimería Alta, and they were going to build and rebuild along the Kino mission chain.

They built at San Ignacio where Kino had stopped his second day in the land. They worked on the hilltops at Pitiquito, Oquitoa, and Cocóspera. A new church rose at Magdalena. The church at Tubutama was finished in 1783, the seventh church to be built on the site. They had grand plans for Tumacácori, a multi-domed church with two towers. In the end, with money and their own time in the territory running out, they finished a smaller church with a single dome and a single tower.

Building materials were local — raw adobe, burnt brick, and rocks for the walls; mesquite wood for the beams, woodwork, staircases, and doors. Inside, the walls were painted and stenciled with the designs of religion and nature. The artists and the statuary were from the interior of Mexico, the muscle and the craftsmanship from the villages.

At the mission of San Xavier del Bac, they did have Espinosa's church, described in a 1772 report as "of medium capacity, adorned with two side chapels in gilded frames." Contemporary site studies indicate the church was rectangular, with an interior containing approximately 1,950 square feet. It would serve until the walls of the new church rose. Then, according to Dr. Bernard Fontana, anthropologist and

San Xavier historian, builders cannibalized usable materials from the old church for other structures at the mission.

The first Franciscan priest to serve at San Xavier was Father Francisco Hermenegildo Garcés, although much of his time was spent in exploration. Garcés' travels to California laid the route for the later expedition of Capt. Juan Bautista de Anza and the founding of San Francisco. Garcés and three other missionaries were killed in 1781 along the Colorado River in a revolt by the Yumas.

The new church of San Xavier del Bac was begun on the watch of Father Juan Bautista de Velderrain around 1783. The priest died in 1790, possibly of typhoid, with his work in progress. The church was completed under the guidance of Father Juan Bautista Llorens in 1797.

In 1804, the *commandante* of the Presidio of Tucson, the fortified community to the north, wrote, "The only public work here that is truly worthy of this report is the church at San Xavier del Bac." The commander, Capt. José Zúñiga, then gave a description of the church, its measurements, and statuary, adding that it existed in part "to attract by its sheer beauty the unconverted Papagos and Gila Pimas beyond the frontier."

By the late 1830s, there would be no priest to greet them. The Franciscans also had been given their marching orders, this time from the newly independent government of Mexico, engaged in the revolutionary turmoil that began in 1810 and extended well into the 20th century. The Spanish-born, including the friars, must leave, declared the government of 1827. Subsequent Mexican governments

and revolutionaries would continue to view the Catholic Church and its minions with a wary eye. Missions were abandoned or left to the infrequent visits of circuit-riding priests. Many of the mission outposts faced the almost ceaseless raids by those who had never come to the religion, the Apaches.

In 1837, Father Antonio Gonzalez, a Mexican-born Franciscan, left his residency at San Xavier del Bac. It would be another 76 years before the men of the Order of Friars Minor would return to live beside the graceful church they had built in the desert.

A Heavenly Tour

John P. Schaefer spent several months in 1977 producing a photoessay of Mission San Xavier del Bac. At the time, he was president of the University of Arizona, and photography was his hobby.

The accompanying photographs were published in his book, *People, Places and Things: Thirty Years in Photography*.

Schaefer titled the images simply: "Door Handle" and "Feet of the Crucified." In his book, Schaefer writes: "Photography is a language and photographs are meant to be read by the viewer."

In taking each photograph, Schaefer focused on a portion of the overall form. Here he draws the eye to the contrasting textures of worn metal and rough wood.

SERPENTINE DOOR HANDLE, MAIN DOOR OF THE CHURCH, 1977. PHOTOGRAPH BY JOHN P. SCHAEFER.

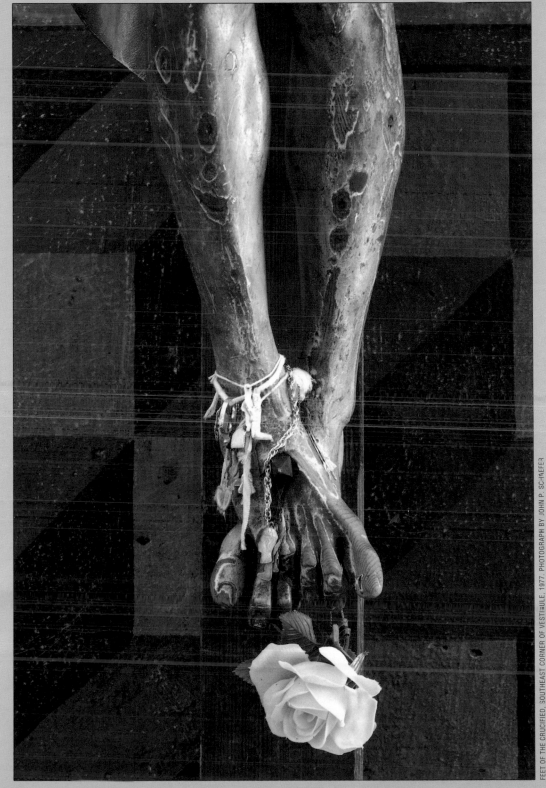

FEET OF THE CRUCIFIED, SOUTHEAST CORNER OF VESTIBULE, 1977. PHOTOGRAPH BY JOHN P. SCHAEFER

RICHARD MAACK

CHAPTER TWO

A Heavenly Tour

"I doubt if even in Europe, with its mystic shrines dating back countless ages, I could have experienced a more profound sense of awe than when standing in that absolutely desert spot, and realizing that skilled hands had once erected there such a monument."

— Mrs. Orsemus Bronson Boyd, 1870
From *Cavalry Life in Tent & Field,* a book on her Arizona travels

THE INTERIOR

In the 1780s, while the walls of San Xavier del Bac were rising in the new world, Mozart was playing in the old one. Immanuel Kant's *Critique of Pure Reason* had just been published, the planet Uranus just discovered. The Age of Enlightenment was at its peak.

During the years when the laborers laid the bricks, created the massive altarpiece, and decorated the domes, French people overthrew their government, slaves rebelled in Santo Domingo, and a man named Washington became president of a country that had been born demanding freedom. Cross San Xavier del Bac's threshold and you enter those last years of the 18th century.

The form of San Xavier is that of a Latin cross, a long center aisle ending in the sanctuary that houses the main altar. Behind it is the *retablo mayor* (pronounced ray-tah-blow my-yore), the gilt framework holding statuary, decorations, and columns.

The transept, the crossbar aisle, has a small chapel at each end. On the east side (on your right as you face front) is the chapel dedicated to Our Sorrowing Mother. On the west side is the chapel of the Suffering Savior. Within each chapel are small altars.

The initial visual impact is one of color, almost riotous: the gold of the altarpiece; the blue, yellow, and red of the geometric step patterns lining the walls; the delicate hues of the niches that house the statues. Every surface seems covered with artworks and designs. Depictions of religious events like the Last Supper have been painted directly on the walls. Lifting the gaze upward are figures drawn on the white backdrop of the arches and domes.

What is not painted is carved, twisted, turned, filled with statues. There are more than 30 statues with full figures in the church and five more on the facade outside.

The interior of San Xavier is a classroom of Catholicism where the history and the tenets of the religion could be taught to the new converts and the yet-to-be-converted. The lesson begins at the highest point of the retablo mayor with God the Father. The very observant and the Gaelic may note he has red hair. His right hand is raised in blessing, his left rests on a globe of the world. Below him is the Immaculate

(ABOVE) *St. Francis of Assisi promoted the virtues of poverty, chastity, and obedience. He is honored as the spiritual father of the Franciscans.*
(RIGHT) *The walls and ceilings of San Xavier are both a classroom of religion and a feast for the eyes. This is one of two full-figure angels on either side of the sanctuary at the entrance to the transepts, which call to mind the horizontal portion of the Latin cross. The Franciscan cord passes over the angel's head.*

JACK DYKINGA

DON STEVENSON

DON STEVENSON

Conception, one of the many images in the church of the Virgin Mother that include a statue in the east chapel and a number of paintings and monograms. Near her, to the viewer's left, is St. Peter; to the right, St. Paul, part of the procession of saints adorning the church.

In the center of the altarpiece, ordered in 1759 by Espinosa, is St. Francis Xavier. Supporting the dome at the edge of the sanctuary are the painted figures of St. Thomas Aquinas, St. Augustine, St. Gregory, and St. Jerome. These men were teachers and scholars of the Catholic faith. St. Ignatius of Loyola, founder of the Society of Jesus, the Jesuits, adorns the column on the edge of the east transept, and St. Dominic, founder of the Order of Preachers, the Dominicans, is in the west

transept, where St. Francis of Assisi has a place of honor.

Below St. Francis is the figure of Christ with his crown of thorns, and below him the reclining figure of St. Francis Xavier, depicting his body as it is enshrined in Goa, India.

Joining the saintly are the sublime, the angels. They are everywhere, choir and orchestra. They blow horns, play violins. They hold back the carved drapery that frames the statues. They frolic on clouds high on the walls. Almost human-sized angels, the bare legged twins, mark each side of the sanctuary with their colorful wings and dancing demeanor. There are the wall-bound torsos of blond-haired angels and headless fair-skinned angels and tiny dark-skinned angels who serve among the saints in the

west transept. Painted, carved, flying, smiling — San Xavier depicts hundreds of angels in a celestial playground.

The angelic vision of the joy of religion is mingled with the pain of it. St. Fidelis stands to the viewer's right on the second tier in the east transept. The Capuchin martyr has both a knife in his chest and a bleeding gash on his head. On the wall near the front door, almost

(LEFT) *A multitude of saints adorns the walls and altars of the mission's ornate interior.*
(CENTER) *One of them, St. Fidelis, is depicted with a knife thrust into his chest.*
(RIGHT) *Another, St. Elizabeth of Portugal, has regal adornment including a crown and scepter. She was the daughter and wife of kings.*

RICHARD MAACK

(ABOVE) *This statue depicts Mary, mother of Jesus, as the Immaculate Conception. The term means that she was born free of original sin.* (RIGHT) *Lions are found both in the church and outside it. This is one of the two at the edge of the sanctuary but it is not original to the church.* (OPPOSITE PAGE) *The art and the architecture draw the visitor into the church and into the gilt and glory of the 18th century.*

hidden, is the figure of Christ on the cross. With toes and fingers broken away, the sores of time add to the horror of the crucifixion. The faithful tie tokens of their belief — rosaries and medals — to the figure.

Only a few feet away is the painting of the Virgin of Guadalupe, who is believed to have appeared to Mexican peasant Juan Diego in 1531. In honor of the miraculous appearance, the Basilica de Guadalupe was built outside Mexico City.

San Xavier's interior is held together, tied together, by the symbol of the cord, the rope belt of the Franciscans. It begins over the choir loft, runs down the center of the walls on either side of the nave, and ends on the retablo, the tassels falling on either side of St. Xavier. The cord also ties together the visual effect of a pleated cloth. From the light brown hem hang pomegranates and bells. This is a visual reference to a passage in Exodus on the clothing of priests: "All around the hem at the bottom you shall make pomegranates, woven of violet, purple and scarlet yarn and fine linen twined, with gold bells between them; first a gold bell, then a pomegranate, and thus alternating all around the hem of the robe."

The Franciscan cord also is seen in the emblem of the order, a cross with the bared arm of Christ and the sleeved arm of St. Francis. The emblem is painted under the first archway near the main door and appears on the outside facade. The cord motif also is carried on the metal chandelier at the entrance.

Another symbol used throughout this church and other Kino missions is the shell. A shell holds the altar. Shells hold the holy water on the walls. A shell cups the balcony on the facade. The shell is a symbol of pilgrimage and the shrine of the patron saint of Spain — Santiago or St. James the Greater. His shrine is located in the sea coast town of Compostela. Pilgrims would carry shells back to their homes as tokens of their visit.

Not all within the church is directly connected to the religion. The grinning lions sitting on the sanctuary rails often have been identified with the banner of Castile, the flag of the Catholic monarchs Isabela and Ferdinand who unified Spain in the late 1400s and sponsored a traveler named Columbus. However, others note the Castilian lions are rampant, rearing up, while the San Xavier lions sit more as guards.

The altar lions are not of the 18th century but of the 20th. The original lions disappeared in 1982. Replacements, very similar to the originals but not replicas, were made in Puebla, Mexico, by men who practice the dying art of carving carousel animals. Installed in 1988, the lions joined a small

JACK DYKINGA

JACK DYKINGA

JACK DYKINGA

(ABOVE) *Here is a rare record identifying one who worked on San Xavier. The abbreviated name carved on the sacristy door with the date of the church's completion stands for Pedro Bojorquez, believed to have been a Spanish soldier working as a carpenter.* (OPPOSITE PAGE) *Other artisans and artists left only marks of their talent, such as the intricate design carved on the wooden pulpit.*

menagerie at San Xavier, the other members far more subtle than the human-fisted lions.

Deer, rabbits, and snails have their own place in the designs along the cornice, the decorated band running along the upper half of the walls. Some of the animals can be seen by looking directly above the lion on the viewer's left. Such drawings are tied to the native workers,

symbols of their land and life outside the walls of the churches. Visitors to the mission of Tumacácori to the south also can see a tiny rooster courting a tiny hen high on the wall above the entrance.

Another desert dweller found a home in the designs of San Xavier. A snake slithers its way along the walls of the sanctuary. Newer reptilian additions from

the second half of the 20th century include the snakes on the handles of the front door.

Little expense was spared in decoration. Statues were ordered from the interior of Mexico. They arrived in parts — heads, feet, hands — and were given body frames. Expensive pigments for a rainbow of colors, including vermilion red and Prussian blue, were ordered from Mexico or Europe. Both gold and silver leaf were covered with transparent, colored lacquers, producing a mother-of-pearl effect.

Artists received twice their normal daily rate, a kind of hazardous duty pay for working in the Empire's outback. And, while the building materials would be local and basic — fired adobe and lime mortar — there were, as reported in 1797 by Father Francisco Iturralde, who was head of the Pimería Alta missions, "four windows in the main body, all complete with their glass window panes, and four more up in the octagonal drum supporting the main dome." Glass window panes were used in a time and place where stretched animal hides were usually the only choice to provide ventilation and protection from the elements.

San Xavier del Bac is a blend of architectural and design styles. The ornate, grand, gilt surfaces of Mexican baroque fuse with the style of *mudejar*, often referred to as Moorish in reference to this church. The mudejar style is the result of the centuries of Islamic influence in Spain, which entered this continent with the conquest of the 1520s. The Mexican architect and art historian Jorge Olvera has pointed out similarities between San Xavier and buildings in the Middle East, including the Dome of the Rock in Jerusalem, also atop an eight-sided drum.

The pilasters, the columns of rectangles and pyramids, are Churrigueresque. Of special interest is that their intricate surfaces are not carved from wood. They, too, like the entire retablo, are made from fired brick and plaster.

Very little is known about the artists and artisans who created the church. One name appears on the sacristy door adjacent to the altar area, that of Pedro Bojorquez with the date of 1797. In the past, he has been named as the possible builder or the artist of the church. However, historian Fontana has stated his belief that Bojorquez may have been a soldier working as a carpenter at San Xavier.

A Spaniard listed on local census rolls of the period is credited as the architect/mason of the church. That person — Ignacio Gaona or Ygnacio Gauna — is also credited with the church of Caborca, one of the original Kino missions. Completed 12 years after San Xavier, the Caborca church is strikingly similar in appearance to its older sister to the north.

The native people, the O'odham for whom the San Xavier was being built, were also the builders — constructing the kilns, firing the bricks, working on the outside and the inside as masons and artisans. They, too, may have left behind a signature of sorts. One source has it that the blue dots that appear on different walls in the church may have been made with their thumbs. At Tumacácori, a member of the park staff believes the pebble

RICHARD MAACK

designs on the outside of that structure are the decorated imprints of the original workers' hands.

Amid all the artistry and beauty, the heavenly expanse of carvings and paintings, the lessons of religion, there is one spot of ignobility inside the church of San Xavier del Bac. Behind the pulpit is a niche where no statue stands. This is the Judas niche, an empty place within these ornate walls for the apostle who betrayed his Lord.

THE EXTERIOR

The white towers and domes of San Xavier del Bac can be seen for miles, from passing cars on the freeway, from a window seat in a jet taxiing to a gate at the city airport. Approached from the south, it is impressive, sitting high at the end of Little Nogales Drive. Historic drawings and photographs show how little this view has been altered from that seen by travelers more than a century ago.

The church is 67 feet wide, 107 feet long. It rises 80 feet above the ground at its highest point, the filigreed cross atop the west bell tower. The ornate facade incorporates the visual elements of the retablo mayor inside with its pilasters and the saint-holding niches. The saint to the viewer's right of the door has long been identified as St. Lucy, a martyr. She is the patron saint for those suffering from eye ailments.

St. Cecilia is above. There is a melancholy irony in the fact that the head of the statue is gone. St. Cecilia is believed to have lived three days after an attempted beheading. She is known as the patron saint of musicians.

Over the years, the identifications of the two statues on the left side of the facade have changed. For a long time, the lower one was identified as possibly being St. Catherine of Siena and the upper one as St. Barbara, killed by her father for her Christian beliefs.

30

In the 1990s, the identifications were changed. Richard Ahlborn of the Smithsonian Institute and Yvonne Lange, specialist in Christian iconography, identified the lower statue as St. Agatha of Catania, who was tortured and killed for her faith, and the upper one as St. Agnes of Rome, the patron saint of chastity martyred at the age of 12 or 13.

On either side of the facade above the female saints are the two lions of Castile. Between them is the two-armed emblem of the Franciscans, and above that is all that remains of the statue of the one male saint on the facade, St. Francis of Assisi. Time has reduced the statue to a sand-colored cone.

The mortuary chapel, built in 1796, is west of the church. The walls surrounding the mortuary carry the stations of the cross, the pictorial steps of Christ to the crucifixion. In the small chapel is a statue of the Virgin Mary always surrounded by candles left by those who come to pray. Beneath the floor are the bones of two Franciscan priests who apparently should be someplace else, and were until 1935.

The final remains of Fathers Narciso Gutiérez and Baltasar Carrillo were at the mission of Tumacácori, where they had served in the 1700s. A 19th century misreading of the records had them down as serving at San Xavier and so the graveyard move was made to their current, if not final, resting place.

As were the other missions, San Xavier was more than church and chapel. The complex housed priests and visitors and provided rooms for mission work and corrals for livestock. With the exception of the corral, the need for supporting structures at San Xavier has remained the same.

The former convento, the residence wing of the 19th century, stretches east-west from the east tower (to your right as you face the facade) and is believed to have been built in the early 1800s, partly with materials from the Espinosa church of the 1750s. The building now houses the mission museum.

A new north-south convento wing was added in the 1900s, and in 1994 the residence now used by the Franciscans was completed to the rear of the complex.

The area that once served as a corral and courtyard is now the inner garden patio. A part of the non-public area of the mission, it can be seen by visitors from the covered veranda off the museum. The view includes that of the Granjon's Gate. This high, sweeping arch with three smaller arches on either side was built in the early 1900s by Bishop Henry

JACK DYK MGA

Granjon and has long been a favorite focal point of photographers.

In addition to the mission buildings at San Xavier, there are the buildings of the O'odham community. To the west of the church are administrative offices for the San Xavier district of the Tohono O'odham's reservation, an elder center, and the school run by the Franciscan Sisters

(ABOVE) *San Xavier's architecture is a blend of styles. This archway view looks southwest to the dome and bell tower, Moorish-influenced hallmarks of Spanish colonial architecture.*
(OPPOSITE PAGE) *An ornate facade decorates the main entrance to San Xavier. Identifications of some figures in the niches have changed over the years, and time has worn away some of the statuary.*

of Christian Charity. The history of the school, like that of the church, began with the Jesuits.

The blackrobes did come back to their mission, in 1863, from California. A fellow traveler in the territory recorded his impressions of the two priests. Wrote journalist J. Ross Browne: "The reverend fathers entertained us during our sojourn with an enthusiastic account of their plans for the restoration of the mission and the instruction and advancement of the Indian tribes with whom they were destined to be associated for some years to come."

He had overestimated the order's second involvement with San Xavier. The priests were gone in a year, called back to California. However, they did make an impact. They established a school at the mission, leading to the first educational appropriation in the Arizona Territory. The sum was $250, allocated by the First Legislative Assembly. By the time the appropriation was approved, the priests were gone. Other schools would open, close, and reopen in the 1870s and 1880s.

(RIGHT) *The full moon seems to mimic the graceful arc of the dome over San Xavier's sanctuary. This is the view from the west side of the church.*

The mission complex and the other buildings can be seen from the hill east of the mission, the hill of the cross. The lions guarding the path to the hill made their own unexpected trip off the premises in 1971. But, unlike their pride brothers inside the church, these lions were returned, no questions asked. Nor, to this day, are they answered. When questioned about the incident decades later, Father Kieran McCarty, pastor at the time of the theft, said only, "I knew they were college kids."

On the hill is the grotto built in 1908 in honor of the appearance of the Virgin Mary at Lourdes, France, in 1858. A statue of the Virgin overlooks the gifts, candles, ribbons, and rosaries left by believers. A path around the top of the hill provides an excellent wraparound view of the Santa Catalina mountains to the north and the city of Tucson to the east.

There are also cement banquettes from which to contemplate both the beauty of the mission below and one of its mysteries: Why wasn't the east tower finished?

As Father Iturralde wrote in 1797, "The church has two towers. One tower remains unfinished — all that is really needed to finish it is a small dome and lantern at the top." That was never to be.

Legends, Myths, and Miracles

Photography is about light and lines just like dancing is, Esther Henderson would say, having left a career as a dancer for one as a photographer.

Her new work brought her to Tucson in the 1930s, and by the end of the decade she was among the photographers helping editor Raymond Carlson make *Arizona Highways* known around the world with premier color photography.

But she did not abandon black and white photography. The accompanying photograph reveals her view that photography is about light and lines. It was taken from the hill east of the mission where decades before Watkins had set up his camera.

She found subjects all over Arizona — neighbors chatting in Prescott, a family celebrating July 4 in Sabino Canyon, Indians in northeastern Arizona, and panoramas in Sedona, the Grand Canyon, and elsewhere.

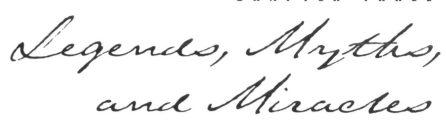
RICHARD MAACK

CHAPTER THREE

Legends, Myths, and Miracles

Stories about San Xavier del Bac have become part of the southern Arizona folklore and are passed on to visitors who come to the church from around the world. Some erroneously have been accepted as fact. Others have moved into the realm of legends. All of them attempt to explain the unexplainable and to fill in the blanks of historical records.

THE UNFINISHED EAST BELL TOWER

One explanation given for the unfinished east bell tower is that the mission was avoiding taxation, that unfinished buildings during the period were not subject to government taxes. However, the fact is that the Spanish missions were not taxed and during much of their existence received government support in the form of small yearly stipends.

There are the tales of the fall — that a priest fell from the tower and so did the architect Gaona. Current research does not indicate the death of a priest in that manner. And, if Gaona took a fatal fall, a true miracle transpired since he is credited with later work at the church of Caborca. Still, the story goes, the native workers refused to finish the tower after the death. Another variation is that the local belief had Gaona turning into a giant rattlesnake after the fall. The snake, it has been said, is still there under the tower and is a powerful incentive in any era to avoid working in the area.

The most probable answer to the riddle of the tower is far more mundane but based on the reality of life at the missions. Then, as now, money was at the heart of major building decisions. The grandiose plans for Tumacácori were never completed, although thousands of the mission's cattle were sold for the project. Money may have run out at San Xavier as well, leaving the one tower to stand unfinished.

THE CAT AND THE MOUSE

For two hundred years, a standoff has taken place on the facade of San Xavier. Perched on either side of the facade within the swirls that mark the edge of the third tier are the mission's antagonists, the cat and the mouse. The elements almost have obliterated the physical differences that originally defined the stone figures. But the cat is to the right, the mouse to the left.

As one story goes, should the cat ever catch the mouse, the

(ABOVE) *As the husband of Mary and one who helped rear Jesus, St. Joseph is a member of the Holy Family. The statue is in the west transept.*
(RIGHT) *The mouse of San Xavier hides in the swirl of a curve on the facade's west side at the church's main entrance. On the east side, in another swirl, a cat waits. The hope is they shall never meet.*

world will end. Tucson folklorist James Griffith relates another oral tradition: that peace will exist between the O'odham and the Spanish until the cat pounces. In fact, peace between the people of San Xavier and the Spanish did continue from 1797 until the end of Spanish rule, a demise that began with the Mexican call to freedom, the Grito de Dolores, in 1810.

THE HOUSE OF THE WIND

In 1699, Capt. Juan Mateo Manje, who accompanied Kino on many of his trips in the Pimería Alta, visited the village of San Xavier with the priest. Father Antonio Leal, who as father visitor supervised and reported on the Pimería Alta missions, was with them.

Manje, Leal, and some soldiers climbed a nearby hill that had a stone wall and a plaza at the top. A later historian speculated it could have been the hill to the southwest of the mission; another said it could have been the hill of the cross to the east.

(RIGHT) *Mysteries concerning the angels on either side of the sanctuary and the lions that guard it add an intriguing element to the elegance evident in the church's statuary. Who were the models, if any, for the angels? What happened to the original lions, stolen in 1982?*

In the center of the hill was a plaza where, wrote Manje, "There was a white stone like a pyre or a sugar loaf, half a vara high (about 16 to 17 inches) and stuck in the ground." Thinking it was an idol, they pulled the stone out and went back down the hill.

"But before we reached the village," Manje recalled, "there arose a great and furious wind and hurricane which hurled us down on the ground, making it impossible to walk on account of the fury and the force with which it blew."

Nature's fury was matched by that of the people of San Xavier who told Manje that the thoughtless action had opened the House of the Wind. The next day, after a wind-filled night, the villagers replaced the stone and the "furious hurricane ceased completely and the day was serene and peaceful."

Manje described it as a "volcano of air," and went on to speculate about earthquakes in the area although the villagers told him there were none in their memory. But there were volcanoes. The walls of San Xavier are full of their rocky remains and one source has it that the O'odham believed the hill of the cross was a true volcano that dried up when the Spanish arrived.

Louis Lopez, teacher of O'odham history and language,

has not heard that story among his people. But he does know of the House of the Wind. According to the Tohono O'odham tradition, it is a mountain located approximately 65 miles west of Tucson. A large rock sits at its top and a constant breeze blows. An old story says there was a time when people thoughtlessly removed the rock, releasing the wind, and others had to go up and return the stone to its rightful place.

THE ANGELS

The two large angels on either side of the altar, with the dancing legs and the hands posed to hold banners, instruments, or other decorative effects, have earned their own bit of legend. A tale once told is that they were modeled after the twin daughters of the artist. But the identities of the artist and his progeny remain unknown.

For those who love a story with a touch of romance, there is a contemporary one to be told about the angels and this tale can be verified.

In 1996, work began to bring the angels back to their original beauty. Decades of neglect, smoke, dirt, and the splattering of bird and bat excrement had taken a serious toll. They were hand-cleaned for eight months. Doing the delicate work were Spanish art conservator Matilde Rubio and apprentice conservator Timothy Lewis. Lewis

LEGENDS, MYTHS, AND MIRACLES

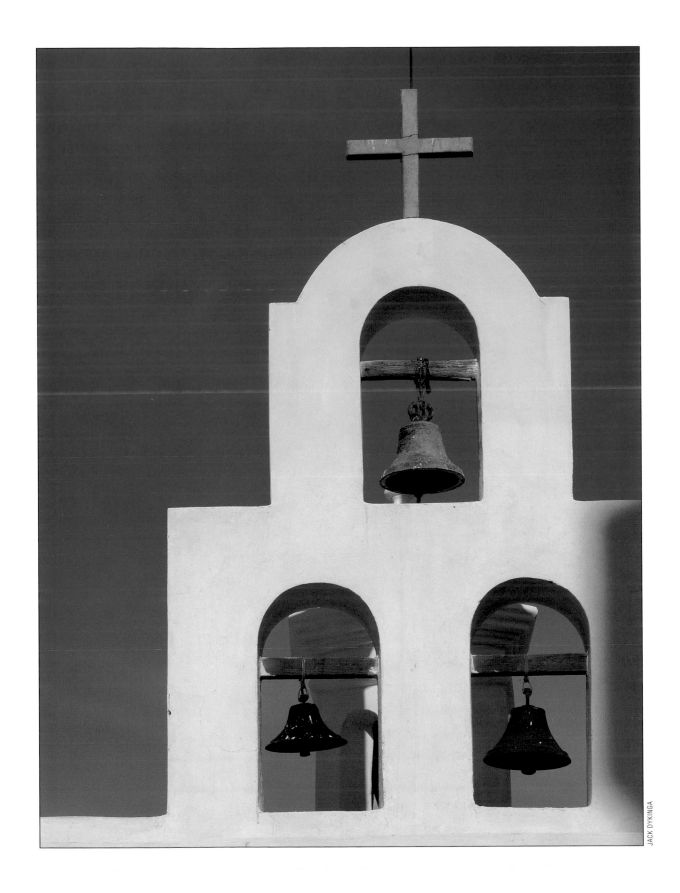

JACK DYKINGA

40

and Rubio met in Europe while working on another project and were married.

Lewis was raised on the San Xavier Reservation and was one of the four local apprentice conservators who worked on the major conservation effort at the church in the 1990s.

HIDDEN TREASURE

One legend definitely made its way across the centuries to the detriment of the Kino missions. The legend of Jesuit gold was the long-held belief that treasures were hidden away before the Jesuits were expelled. The stories were told from Baja California to Sonora and Arizona that church bells were made of gold, that the priests were mining silver, that tunnels led out of the missions, that hidden caves near them were filled with treasure guarded by loyal converts. The legend existed in the Empire's urban areas as well. Jesuit colleges, headquarters of the order, were ransacked, and graves desecrated when the priests left.

A Jesuit who had served the missions decried this belief years after the expulsion and his own imprisonment in Spain. Wrote Father Ignaz Pfefferkorn, "I ask only the question, 'What did we missionaries do with this astonishing collection of gold and silver?'"

"There simply wasn't any," says Father Charles Polzer, Jesuit and historian of the mission period. "Most of these stories were concocted by people at a later time."

Unfortunately for the missions, there have always been believers in the hidden treasure

JACK DYKINGA

yet to be found. Treasure hunters tore through walls at Tumacácori and reduced Cocóspera to rubble, leaving the land around it as cratered as a World War I battleground. San Xavier, like San Ignacio and Tumacácori, was said to have one of those secret tunnels but was spared the destruction of a useless search.

In reality, the missions never overflowed with riches. A 1768 inventory at San Xavier does list silver altar vessels, candlesticks, and a "little silver bell." But they were balanced by a doleful list of living essentials. They included "an old, broken and useless small copper pot," which went with the 10 forks and spoons, "one of them broken." They did have "two old chairs" and two cots, but the cots were "useless because they are torn." Even with four candles, a writing desk, one salt shaker, and "two old iron pans," the mission did not qualify as a treasure trove.

The real treasure of the Pimería Alta and the rest of the Empire was in the mines. A discovery of legendary proportions was made at Arizonac, 70 miles south of Tucson. There, in the 1730s, a lump of silver was found, its weight given as 2,500 pounds. Smaller but no less impressive balls of silver said to weigh up to 60 pounds also were found. The ore was so pure that there was speculation that it might be the "Treasure of Montezuma," another legend.

As for the Jesuits, they didn't do the mining, and they protected the people of the missions from the horror of working in the mines, be that for humanitarian or proprietary reasons. Even if there was treasure to hide, there was little time to do so. The expelled priests were barely given time to dress before they were force-marched out of the territory.

It can be noted that bells still hang, dark and heavy, at San Xavier and other missions in the Pimería Alta. For over a century and a half they have been examined by any number of soldiers, travelers, bandits, and vagabonds and then left

(OPPOSITE PAGE) *The bells of San Xavier's mortuary chapel are not made of gold as legend might have it.*
(ABOVE) *Cocóspera, a Kino mission in Sonora, was ravaged by frustrated looters. There was no treasure to find. Fortunately, San Xavier was spared such depredations.*

behind. Serviceable they may be, possibly even melodious, but not made of gold.

THE MIRACULOUS

San Xavier has been the site of at least one recorded "miraculous" event, the death of a Franciscan who arrived at the mission in June, 1802. Father Ignacio Joseph Ramírez y Arellano was a son of Mexico from the province of Puebla southeast of Mexico City. He is known in the history of San Xavier for two things, his letters to his family and his death.

In his letters, he wrote of the abundance of the land of San Xavier. "Get on a saddle some afternoon and come here for a ride and you will eat good watermelons and cantaloupes, peaches, grapes, pomegranates, and a thousand other things." He wrote of the power of nature, the great storms

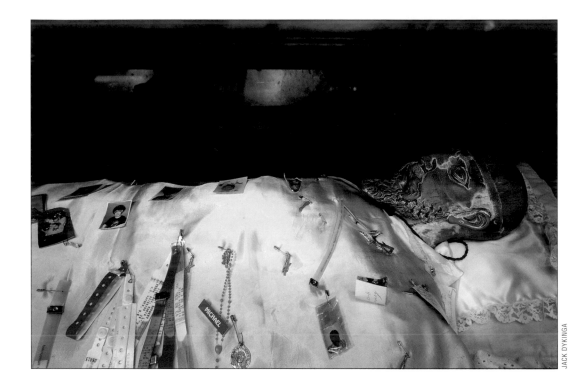

JACK DYKINGA

(ABOVE) The coverlet of the statue of San Xavier is covered with tokens left by those in need of a milagro, *a miracle. Others have left behind pictures, medical bracelets, and rosaries as a gift in return for an answered prayer.*
(OPPOSITE PAGE) *The statue on the facade's lower right depicts St. Lucy, an Italian woman denounced by her fiancé as a Christian and forced to work in a brothel early in the 4th century. Eventually she was martyred.*

that rumbled across the desert. "What noises. What thunder. What wind. It appears that these elements wish to lift us and the house up to the stars."

Father Ignacio was struck with a fever in September 1805. He was dead within a few weeks. For hours after his death, his body continued sweating and omitting, it was said, a sweet odor. People came out from Tucson to witness the "miracle." Once the body returned to a more natural state of death, Father Ignacio was buried.

Modern speculation includes typhoid as the possible cause of death and no doubt a medical

reason could be put forth as to the cause of the sweating and sweet odor. But the strength of religion is not built on earth-bound explanations. The possibility of a miracle, an answered prayer, a reversal of fortune, resides in San Xavier as it does in the hearts of the faithful.

Every day at the church, those who believe, who need, who wish to offer thanksgiving as well as request a favor, approach the reclining statue of St. Xavier in the west transept. Upon the statue's coverlet, they pin *milagros*, little metal charms depicting parts of the body for which they need help or a cure. There are tiny legs, arms, a head, a heart. Pictures of loved

ones, medical bracelets, and notes are also left. "Please help us find the way" was the written request on one day. "Please let our son return" was another.

Other offerings are made in the mortuary chapel, rosary beads hung around the neck of the statue of the Virgin, photographs placed on the altar before her. Pictures of school children, babies, snapshots of automobile accidents with the names of the survivors written on the back sit amid the candles lit in her name.

The statues themselves are not viewed as powerful. The reverence is for the individuals represented by the statues. These individuals are associated with certain worldly interests often connected with events in their own lives. For example, St. Bernardine of Feltre's statue is found in the east transept. He helped to establish a loan system that allowed the poor to borrow money at low rates. He has become a patron of pawnbrokers and bankers.

Local stories have developed around the statues themselves. The reclining St. Francis Xavier has no legs. Unlike other statues that never had legs, his lower limbs appear to have been cut off. One oral tradition is that raiding Apaches did the chopping, but there is a story with a gentler touch.

At the church of Magdalena in Sonora, Mexico, there is a similar statue of St. Xavier. James Griffith tells of a belief that the two statues once traded places and St. Francis Xavier wore his legs off on the trek up from Mexico. Now, after Sunday mass, a long line of people slowly passes by the statue. Some stop and place a hand underneath its neck, then lift the head, an indication of their faith or of the favorable outcome of a request. They may not know the statue was given cloth legs in 1996 by an art conservator working at the mission. It probably wouldn't matter. Many of these people have walked their own hard road. In legend or belief, this saint has walked beside them.

The People of San Xavier

The Buehman Studio in Tucson photographed individuals, scenes, and everyday events from the 1870s, when Henry Buehman bought the studio, to the 1950s.

In 1875, Buehman traveled through Arizona to record people and scenes. His stops included Camp Bowic, Camp Grant, and the San Carlos Indian Reservation. He first added San Xavier to his subjects in 1876.

In about 1895 he recorded at the mission's main entrance three men sporting a relatively new method of transportation. In the same era, he photographed nuns with their pupils, the children on whose ancestral land the church had been built.

RICHARD MAACK

CHAPTER FOUR

The People of San Xavier

TOHONO O'ODHAM

here is a point in the Catholic Mass, the daily service at San Xavier, when members of the congregation turn to each other, shaking the hands of those nearest, and say, "Peace be with you." Tourists find themselves drawn in, included in the welcoming smiles and extended hands. Some look startled, confused. Many visitors do not realize that this is an active church, a parish church of the Tohono O'odham.

The Spanish called them Papagos, probably a corruption of the Piman word for bean eater or bean people. They are part of the Piman linguistic group, the ancient people, the O'odham, who lived in the desert and along the rivers of the Pimería Alta. In 1986, those of the desert banished the Papago label to the past, making it official. They were the Tohono O'odham, the Desert People.

When Kino arrived, the Tohono O'odham were semi-nomadic, two-village people living near the mountains in the winter, in the desert in the warm months. While modern travelers may find that a strange choice, the Tohono O'odham knew that the desert could and did provide for its people. There was cactus to be harvested in the spring and summer — the fruit of the giant saguaro, the pads of the prickly pear, the buds of the cholla. They picked wild spinach and the pods of the mesquite tree, and they hunted deer and rabbit. One-village O'odham, who lived along the rivers, grew beans, melons, squash, corn, cotton, and tobacco, farming long before the Spanish introduced their wheat and fruit-bearing trees.

The aboriginal population of the Tohono O'odham has been estimated at 12,000. Today, the tribal enrollment is about 20,000 with 60 percent living on the reservation west and south of San Xavier. More than 2,800,000 acres, it is equivalent in size to Connecticut. Kitt Peak National Observatory, southwest of Tucson, is within its boundaries.

The reservation does not include any part of Mexico. That Tohono O'odham land and its people were cut away in 1854 with the ratification of the Gadsden Purchase, in which the United States paid $10 million to Mexico for land including what now is southern Arizona.

But much of the land and the look of it has remained

(ABOVE) *Anthony of Padua, often depicted holding the Christ child, was a popular Franciscan who labored in Italy in the 13th century.*

(RIGHT) *The native people of the Pimería Alta continue to practice the faith brought to them by Father Kino. Ansel Adams recorded this pageant in which young Tohono O'odham participants carry a statue of St. Francis of Assisi. The photograph was a part of Adams' photoessay published in* Arizona Highways *in April 1954.*

48

unchanged over the centuries. Great open expanses of cactus and brush reach southwest toward the Sea of Cortés where the Tohono O'odham once made their pilgrimages for salt. There are horizons so empty you almost believe you see the curvature of the earth. Others are serrated by blue-black mountains. Cattle and horses graze along the slim gray band of highway that leads in and out of the town of Sells, the headquarters of tribal government. That road to Sells runs along the same route that Kino once rode.

The Tohono O'odham, like all other native people of the Pimería Alta, had their own ancient belief system and rituals, many directly related to the land and the animals and plants upon it. The path to a new religion would not be smooth for those expecting to lead the way nor for those expected to follow. As Franciscan historian Father Kieran McCarty points out, life for the priests in the Pimería Alta "was plenty hard, some lost their lives." But, he adds, "… you can throw in an equal time clause there and say the missions weren't so easy on the Indians either."

Old traditions were supposed to be discarded, old rituals traded in for new ones. Some of the missionaries were harsh, inflexible. They despaired

over the plural marriages, bemoaned the ritual drunkenness that was part of the ancient ceremony to bring the rain. Accusations were made against O'odham men who knew the sacred ways and songs, the medicine men, charges of priests being bewitched, poisoned. One Jesuit recommended sending the "bad" inhabitants of San Xavier to the workhouses of Mexico City.

However, there was also more than a century of complimentary reports, beginning

with Kino, who found the native people "affable" and hardworking. "Gentle" is another of the adjectives used in historic record and echoed by today's Tohono O'odham in their own writing. They were known and remain so for their hospitality and their love of giving gifts. They were, after all, the rightful hosts on the land.

"In accordance with their custom, they made us presents," wrote Manje after a visit with Kino to the people of San Xavier.

Be they gentle, hospitable,

and giving, the Tohono O'odham were not without convictions nor the ability to stand and fight for them. They did join other native peoples in the uprisings against the missionaries and the Spanish in 1695

(OPPOSITE PAGE) *Fireworks outshine the lights of Tucson in the celebration of the bicentennial of the church's completion.*
(ABOVE) *At another festival, bonfires light the way.*

JACK DYKINGA

and 1751. They fought back against the Apaches and their raids, matching scalp for scalp.

The Desert People did become Christians and today are predominately Catholic. It is a Tohono O'odham who opens the doors of San Xavier in the morning, and village elders who tend to the statues, change their robes and dresses, and collect the *milagros*. Tohono O'odham of the village of Wa:k are baptized and married at San Xavier, although the numbers are not great. When Kino and his brothers served, thousands received the sacraments bringing them into the faith. In a recent year at San Xavier there were six marriages and 129 baptisms.

That the church still stands as it does, that the statues still exist within, is due in good part to the loyalty of the Tohono O'odham. During the years when San Xavier was all but abandoned, the priests gone, the Mexican government distrustful of any clerical power, the O'odham remained near its walls. They hid away its few treasures — the chalices, cruets, candlesticks, and sanctuary carpet — to be brought out only when the priests returned. Travelers through the territory recorded their impressions of the beauty and decay of San Xavier during the mid-1800s and of the people who protected it.

In 1864, Judge Joseph Allyn, one of the first justices on the Supreme Court of the Territory of Arizona, wrote, "The Papagos or baptized Indians have watched and guarded the fine old pile with rare fidelity."

The strength of a new faith did not erase the values of the old one. The Tohono O'odham do not forget. Every year, in the months of June and July, before the rains begin, they go to the groves of the saguaro, some not far from the mission of San Xavier. From their cactus camps, they harvest the ruby red fruit that crowns the cactus limbs, some up to 30 feet high.

The work is hard and hot for little product but the fruit has many uses. The pulp can be made into jam, the seeds ground into flour. Boiled, the juice becomes a subtle sweet syrup. Fermented, it becomes a wine that is an integral part of the rain ceremony. The rains do come, after the harvest, in the late days of summer, an ancient blessing on the land and its people.

PILGRIMS

San Xavier del Bac is also a spiritual home for the new desert people. On the faces of its congregation can be seen the history of the settlement of Arizona. Those whose veins still carry the blood of Spain and Mexico have never been

far from the church their religion built. These descendants of the original colonists and later immigrants to southern Arizona attend services at San Xavier del Bac. Joining them are the most recent arrivals, people from around the country and the world who have moved to this fast-growing southwestern state and have chosen to become part of the family of the old desert church.

Some make a weekly Sunday visit from the northern cities and towns of Arizona. Some come up from the south, from mining and ranching towns. Some families make a trip to San Xavier part of a yearly reunion, traveling from other states.

For many, the church is an important point of pilgrimage. These are the people who stand in the slow-moving line, waiting for their moment with St. Francis Xavier, the people who light the candles. "One for God and one for San Francisco," one young man explains in Spanish of the two candles he holds. When asked if his prayers are answered, he nods yes.

The pilgrims come with their *mandas*, promises or vows, and leave with hope. They also come

(LEFT) *Candles in the mortuary chapel light the night. Left by worshippers, the flames represent prayers and promises.*

as a way to pay back that which has been given in answer to their prayers.

"Pago la manda," historian Raquel Rubio-Goldsmith explains, using the words of a pilgrim. "I fulfill the vow." She remembers her grandmother's trips to San Xavier from the southeastern Arizona mining town of Douglas on the Mexican border.

"She always had mandas," she recalls. In addition to her own mandas, her grandmother would collect the mandas of her friends. Not everyone could afford to make the trip to Tucson. There were times well into the 20th century when even a drive from Tucson would be beyond the means of a believer. Then, there could be another pilgrimage, a nine-mile walk from city to church. Pilgrims still make that trip, walking alone or in pairs along the two-lane road through the reservation.

While some will go to the grotto or the mortuary chapel, the major drawing card is St. Xavier. "Because he is so miraculous," says Rubio-Goldsmith. There is faith in his ability to cure illness, to help someone find work, to find the loved one who is lost, to answer the pleas written on the tiny notes that fall on the saint's coverlet like flower petals.

"Please, I pray you hear me" are the words of many.

Those who believe take their prayers and their mandas to the mission church of Magdalena in Sonora as well. The week of October 4 marks a major pilgrimage with people from both sides of the border making their way to the town of Magdalena de Kino in honor of the feast of St. Francis of Assisi.

John Bartlett, U.S. boundary commissioner, traveled through the area in the early 1850s and wrote then of the pilgrims who "with their hands crossed on the breasts, advance on their knees a hundred feet or more to the church." Once inside, they would make an offering to a reclining statue of San Francisco (St. Francis), as they still do.

The thousands who travel to Magdalena go with reverence for both St. Francis of Assisi and St. Francis Xavier, the saints having become somewhat intertwined over the years of worship. Father Kino, whose grave is on the edge of the church plaza under a clear dome, is also honored. He died here in 1711, having come to Magdalena to dedicate a chapel. He had built it in the name of, once again, St. Francis Xavier, a pilgrim's saint.

TOURISTS AND OTHER TRAVELERS

Tourists have made San Xavier del Bac a destination or stopping-off place on their own pilgrimages through the American Southwest. An estimated 200,000 to 300,000 people visit the church every year. Arizona residents make their trips to the mission time and time again.

Incredibly, the small church absorbs the visitors, making them, for a few moments at least, part of the people of San Xavier. There have been those unfortunate incidents when loud voices have interrupted church services. But, again, some enter the church thinking it is a museum, albeit one without an admission charge.

The tourist trail to the doors of San Xavier is an old one. The first Anglo Americans in the area were spotted in Tucson in 1826 — three mountain men. But the influx of travelers from the young country to the north did not begin until the 1840s.

They were passing through, always on their way to somewhere else. Soldiers were marching to war and back from one. Would-be millionaires were tromping across to reach the gold-filled rivers of California, surveyors and boundary commissioners a few steps behind. Stagecoaches brought adventurers; the Army brought the wives. A few stopped long enough to visit the church and record their thoughts in journals and letters.

In 1846, the Mormon Battalion marched to Tucson from Santa Fe on its way to California. The war with Mexico had begun and California was enemy territory. So was Tucson. The troops marched in, and the Mexican troops took haven at San Xavier. The U.S. forces marched on to California. Their leader, Lt. Col. Philip St. George Cooke, did make note of the "large stone church" to the south.

In 1848, another Army column moved through on its way to California. The war with Mexico had finally ended, and California was now part of the United States, a piece of the victor's spoils under the terms of the Treaty of Guadalupe Hidalgo. Lt. Cave Johnson Couts wrote about the trek through southwestern Arizona,

(OPPOSITE PAGE) *In the baptistery room off the main church, sunshine warms the old statue of El Nazareno while votive candles lit by the faithful* (ABOVE) *bring their own warmth to the altars and statues of the mission.*

which was still a part of the Republic of Mexico.

He was underwhelmed by Tucson, describing it as "no great deal at all." Tumacácori was noted as "a very large and fine church." But, oh, San Xavier. " 'Tis truly a noble and stupendous building," he wrote.

For Bartlett, the head of the United States Boundary Commission, San Xavier in the early 1850s was "the most beautiful church in the State of Sonora."

Writer J. Ross Browne had some problems with the Arizona of the 1860s. "Mines without miners and forts without soldiers are common. Politicians without policy, traders without trade, store-keepers without stores, teamsters without teams, and all without means," he wrote. But he did like the church, finding it "a splendid monument of civilization."

In 1865, the people of Hartford, Connecticut, were able to do some traveling of their own to San Xavier from the comfort of their armchairs. The evening paper was carrying articles by Judge Joseph Allyn. His words were, no doubt, a welcome respite from the horrors of the Civil War, which finally was coming to an end.

(RIGHT) *Simple crosses mark the graves of the Tohono O'odham. To the east is their church, built for them and by them.*

He wrote, "A prettier sight rarely greets the eye; there was the grand old church, the adobe walls of the old mission garden, the Indian town, the broad irrigated fields, the moving herds, all forming a picture that one would not soon forget."

Mrs. Orsemus Bronson Boyd did not forget it. In 1894, her memories of her travels as the wife of a cavalry officer in the Arizona of the 1870s were published. She was uninformed about the history of the mission, believing the people who once worshipped at San Xavier were unknown and surmised to be "ancient Aztecs, or followers of Montezuma," but the building captivated her.

"I could hardly tear myself from the spot, and returned again and again to ascend the belfry stairs and wonder and speculate upon the strange mystery called San Xavier del Bac."

Tucson, however, was still in great need of a civic booster. Boyd found it "an insignificant town of flat mud houses, so unprepossessing that we were glad to drive throughout without stopping." She had another reason besides the adobe architecture. At the time, the citizens of the town were dealing with the end of a smallpox epidemic, one of the many diseases that periodically swept through the territory.

"A howling wilderness" is how Phocion Way described it in his 1858 diary. He was surprised that San Xavier could have ever been built in such a place. Although, he did predict, "If this country should ever again become thickly populated, it will be renovated and repaired and again used as a place of worship."

The church was already in need of care, if not serious repairs. Despite praise-filled accounts and jaw-dropping impressions of the church in the midst of land so many found devoid of any other beauty, San Xavier was showing the results of years of neglect.

Way had written of birds nesting on the statues. Allyn's articles included references to the "ravages of time upon the noble old pile." He wrote of the defacement by man, "that cosmopolitan sacrilege of scribbling your name on every such famous old monument." Graffiti.

In his account of travels through Arizona in 1870, John Marion, editor of the *Arizona Daily Miner* in Prescott, reported that the figures on the facade were "fast going to decay," as were parts of the roof and the walls.

"This decay ought to be stopped," was his pronouncement, "and the grand old edifice preserved in all its splendor." That work had already begun.

Preserving the Past

HENRY BUEHMAN. ARIZONA HISTORICA. SOCIETY/TUCSON. AHS 20272.

Photographs by Henry Buehman and his son, Albert, show damage and disrepair at San Xavier in two different centuries.

Work to maintain San Xavier began in the years before the American Civil War but the mission was to fall into disrepair again. One enemy of the old structure was nature. In 1887 an earthquake destroyed the garden walls (above) and Henry Buehman chronicled the damage.

An archway (right) built in the first decade of the 20th century eventually showed signs of age by the late 1930s, as recorded here by Albert Buehman. Repairs and preservation continued throughout the 20th century, and when Ansel Adams photographed at the arch (see page 67), it was restored to its initial grandeur.

RICHARD MAACK

CHAPTER FIVE

Preserving the Past

A TOUCH OF FRANCE

nch by painstaking inch, the European and Tohono O'odham conservators worked quietly. They sat on stools or stood hugging the walls of the old church. The tools they used were small — bits of tissue, cotton swabs, syringes.

One man was tapping on a wall, listening for a hollow echo. Sighing, he said, "The earthquake didn't help any."

It is 1997, the end of a six-year project to bring San Xavier's interior back to the glory of 1797. The earthquake he meant took place more than 100 years ago.

Nature has not been kind to San Xavier del Bac. The effects of that earthquake, of two centuries of weather that alternately bakes and freezes, of the power of the rain when it does fall, of lightning that comes with the summer storms, have left their marks. People have done their best to erase them. That work of building, restoring, and preserving the mission has been going on since 1859.

That work began with a series of French priests.

With the last strip of Arizona coming into the United States in 1854, jurisdiction for the mission of San Xavier was turned over to the Diocese of Santa Fe, New Mexico, and Bishop Lamy, whom Willa Cather brought to literary fame in her 1927 book, *Death Comes for the Archbishop.* A secondary character in the novel was a priest described as "short, skinny and bow-legged from a life on horseback, and his countenance had little to recommend it but kindliness and vivacity."

In the book, he was Father Joseph Vaillant who was heading south "to hunt for lost Catholics … utterly lost Catholics … towards Tucson." In reality, he was Father Joseph Projectus Machebeuf, sent to Arizona by Lamy. What he found were San Xavier del Bac and the Tohono O'odham, who brought out the sacred vessels they had saved for this occasion. On a visit to the area in 1859, he began repairs at the mission. Leaks in the roof had damaged the frescoes, and the walls needed to be braced. When he left, Machebeuf wrote, "It could be used for services." He was then sent to Colorado where he would become the first bishop of Denver.

Father Jean Baptiste Salpointe arrived in Tucson in 1866 and began building a church in the city. At San Xavier he began the school, repairing rooms for classes and the nuns who would teach pupils.

(ABOVE) *These angels, depicted heralding a message, help adorn a supporting column in the main altarpiece, the retablo mayor.*
(RIGHT) *In the 1990s, scaffolding filled the church during a major preservation effort. Work to repair, restore, and preserve San Xavier has been ongoing since the return of the priests in the late 1850s.*

58

He is credited with writing a pamphlet on the mission with the proceeds to be used to help complete St. Mary's Hospital in Tucson.

After a robbery in 1880 he announced that there would be an admission fee of 50 cents to see the mission — a pricey ticket, considering that bacon was then being advertised at 10 cents a pound. Salpointe left Tucson as a bishop in 1885 and succeeded Lamy as archbishop.

The next bishop of Tucson, Peter Bourgade, faced a vicarage he described as being 60,000 Catholics in an area the size of France with but 20 priests to serve their spiritual needs. He had a church in Tucson that needed to be replaced and a mission that needed work. Then he had an earthquake.

It rolled into Tucson at 2:12 on the afternoon of May 3, 1887. Rocks came crashing off the Santa Catalina Mountains; homes and buildings were damaged. The epicenter was in northeast Sonora, where 40 died. Shock waves were felt 400 miles away, in New Mexico and Texas, as well as Arizona. A Tucson newspaper reported that rumors of an accompanying volcano were unsubstantiated. But the earthquake had been enough for San Xavier. It shook the walls fencing the mission grounds and brought them down. Further damage was done to the interior, including a large crack in the west transept and damage to the domes. Outside, pilasters had been knocked off the facade.

The church was in "deplorable" condition, recalled a nun who served there. It was infested with bats, and snakes were no longer relegated to wall decorations. By 1892, the front wall was about to cave in and the bishop was collecting money to cover the leaking roof. In addition to the work at the mission, Bourgade was busy finishing a cathedral in Tucson.

In 1899, Bourgade left for new duties as archbishop of Santa Fe.

Now came the builder, Bishop Henry Granjon. In 1906, the *Arizona Daily Star* reported he had been working for 30 days at San Xavier with a budget of $2,000 to complete repairs expected to take another two months. Years of work and $11,000 later, Granjon had finished.

He had added a wing on the east side of the mission complex, built the massive archway, built

(RIGHT) *The white glow of the domes and curves of the church earned it the nickname of "White Dove of the Desert." Fortunately, a suggestion to cover the roof with copper was ignored in 1906. Decades later, an ancient formula would be used as a protective coating.*

PRESERVING THE PAST   *61*

the grotto, covered the unfinished tower with mortar, added walls, put lion heads (since replaced) atop arched outer walls, and put the lions on the path to the hill of the cross. His work was at an end in 1912, when jurisdiction was once again turned over to the Franciscans. Repairs as well as deterioration continued.

A lightning strike damaged the west tower in 1939. In the 1950s, Father Celestine Chinn directed repair efforts, including the replacement of the pilasters on the facade. All but two had been destroyed over the years. Today, the facade has only cement replicas.

Problems continued with the leaking roof. In 1906, two architects, hired by the local chamber of commerce to study the condition of the mission, suggested the roof and domes be covered with copper. Granjon is believed to have quashed that rather startling idea. Later repairs were done with cement. While it didn't have an eye-jarring effect on the outside of the building, it did have an effect on the inside. The

(ABOVE) Prickly pear pads are boiled, then squeezed in a mop wringer by Tony Lopez. The resulting juice provides a necessary ingredient for the formula used to mortar the walls of the old mission.

people of the next major preservation effort would have to deal with it. They would need a new formula for a material to cover the roof and domes, or a very old one.

THE FORMULA

Like his father and grandfather before him, Sonny Morales works on the walls, the domes, the patios of San Xavier. "I look forward to coming to work here every single day," he says. The fourth generation of Moraleses works beside him, his son Danny. The fifth is learning, Danny's sons, Sonny's grandsons.

Morales is the keeper and the maker of the formula for the mortar that holds San Xavier del Bac together. The recipe is simple enough, only three ingredients: lime, sand, and a glue made from cactus juice.

The formula came to the continent with the Spanish conquest as did the type of prickly pear cactus from which the juice is drawn. Nopal de Macho has large flat pads, smooth with no long needles. Using it in a mortar is an old technique. "It could go back 800 years," says Robert Vint, architect for San Xavier during the 1990s preservation project. Cactus juice mortar provides what Vint calls a "breathing skin." Cement does not.

The cement used at different times throughout the repair

work of the 20th century was an incompatible material for the soft brick structure. It gave validity to the architect's axiom, "Soft is always sacrificed to the hard."

Under the fluctuating weather conditions of the Sonoran Desert, the winter cycles of freeze and thaw, the cement used on the roof and domes of the church moved and cracked. Water seeped in and spread to

the brick. Then, when unable to breathe out to the exterior surfaces, it moved to the inside surfaces, damaging the walls, paintings, and decorations.

One of the hardest layers of cement was laid on the church's roof in the 1950s. Forty years later, Morales and his workers peeled it away with chisels and replaced it with the cactus juice mortar. Morales had started working with the

DCN STEVENSON

The years did rest heavy on the interior of San Xavier as it approached its bicentennial decade. The good news, according to Fontana, was that about 80 percent of the decorations had not been lost. The bad news was they were blurred by smoke, dirt, and the touches, sweat, and breath of tens of thousands of people. The statues were covered with the excrement of birds and bats. Well-meaning attempts to restore and preserve had left paintings with a coat of varnish that had blackened over the years. Yes, the decorations, colors, and lines of the 18th century were there, if only they could be seen.

In 1992, seven art conservators — five from Italy, one from Turkey, one from England — began work at San Xavier. They were assisted by Tohono O'odham and directed by Paul Schwartzbaum, chief conservator and assistant director for technical services at New York's Solomon R.

formula as a teenager. Extracting the juice to make it had not been easy.

"We'd get a big drum and we'd put the pads in and we'd smash them with a two-by-four," he remembers. There had to be a better way.

He could boil the pads, but the juice still had to be extracted. Morales tried a hamburger press. He tried squeezing the pads with two hinged boards.

That worked but the juice would soften the wood and loosen the screws. He found the answer at a swap meet in the form of an old mop bucket with its metal squeezer. Attaching the squeezer to a wheelbarrow, he had his prickly pear press.

The pads for the San Xavier mortar must be fresh and moist. First, they are boiled in a cauldron over a wood fire.

Then they are squeezed. Sixty cactus pads produce about eight gallons of light, slightly oily juice.

The mortar consists of four parts sand, one part lime, and one part juice. The replacing of the cement topping on San Xavier required up to 25 coats of cactus juice mortar. But it will last, says Morales, "forever, for years and years and years." The old ways work.

(LEFT) An artisan carries out painstaking, detailed work to remove the scars of time and preserve a painting inside Mission San Xavier. Through much of the 1990s, art conservators worked to remove grime and bring paintings back to their original splendor.

DON STEVENSON

The preservation project was organized and supported by the Patronato San Xavier, a volunteer nonprofit group dedicated to the preservation of the mission. The six years of work cost more than $2 million, raised through private and corporate donations.

Scars did remain. On some of the domes only faint outlines, memories of the patterns, are left. The saints and angels are faded, broken in places. But, overall, the results of the cleaning of San Xavier were astonishing. The dulling of 200 years fell away. The depth and intricacies of the altarpiece, the circus-like colors of the wall decorations, the lines of the paintings were clear again. San Xavier del Bac glowed.

On the evening of April 12, 1997, a party marked the 200th birthday of San Xavier and the winding down of the latest preservation project. Tohono O'odham set off a fireworks display over their old church and rang its bells. Again and again, man-made stars exploded, showering golds and greens and reds into the night sky to the oohs and aahs of those below.

On a nearby hill, one man worked, intent on his own effort to preserve San Xavier. He wasn't using a hammer or a trowel or a swab dabbed in cleaning solution. He was using a camera.

Guggenheim Museum. He was quoted as saying, "In the United States, this is as close as any building comes to the Sistine Chapel. No other Spanish-period church in the United States equals the mission's architecture and art."

The task of the conservators was not to restore but to preserve the beauty of San Xavier. Missing fingers and toes were not replaced on the statues; no new heads for the angels, nor bright new colors for the paintings and niche designs. The interior surfaces were cleaned with water and denatured alcohol. The whites of the walls were toned down with a neutral watercolor, making the remaining color decoration more vivid in comparison. The tiny flakes of paint that had pulled away were glued back to the walls and statues.

Surprises lurked under the layers of dirt. That St. Fidelis had a knife in his chest was obvious, but until the years of droppings were cleaned away no one knew that he also had a gash in his head. The painting long viewed as that of *El Buen Pastor*, the Good Shepherd, was found to be that of Mary, *La Divina Pastora*.

(ABOVE) An art conservator works in the east transept at the base of a niche designed to hold a statue.
(RIGHT) The retablo mayor was designed to be more than just a work of art. Glowing with color, its depiction of God the Father and the saints is a visual tool, teaching tenets of the Catholic faith.

A Visual Legacy

For photographers, Mission San Xavier offers a compelling image of light, shadow, and form, and of history, faith, and strength. Ansel Adams' image (right) embraces all of those qualities.

Adams produced several major photoessays of the mission, including one published in *Arizona Highways* in April 1954. This photograph, showing the refurbished north court arches, is work Adams did in 1968.

Adams first shot at Yosemite, with a Kodak Brownie, in 1916. He was 14. In the 1970s, having become the preeminent American landscape photographer, he donated his archives to help found Tucson's Center for Creative Photography at the University of Arizona.

RICHARD MAACK

CHAPTER SIX

A Visual Legacy

Cameras came with the territory. They were carted in, on the backs of horses, in the backs of wagons, hanging off the backs of the practitioners of the relatively new art. At the end of the Civil War, photographers were moving across the American West documenting the new lands for science, government, and the folks back home. By the early 1870s, their equipment was set up inside and outside San Xavier del Bac.

The names of some of the early local photographers are known. Out of Tucson came the Buehmans, a family of photographers who would operate a studio in that city for 76 years, shooting everything and everyone who stood still. Camillus S. Fly, the pioneer photographer with the gallery in Tombstone, took his shots at San Xavier. Fly's other subjects included the places and personalities of the O.K. Corral era and the Apache wars. He recorded the peace negotiations in 1886 between Geronimo and Gen. George Crook.

Two noted photographers, Carleton Watkins and Timothy O'Sullivan, also made images of San Xavier.

Earlier visitors to the mission sketched or painted it. Sketches were made by forty-niner H.M.T. Powell. Henry C. Pratt, the artist traveling with the Bartlett boundary commission, sketched and painted at San Xavier. A drawing of San Xavier was part of a report for the U.S. Senate on the best route for a railroad line from the Mississippi to the Pacific. Californian J. Ross Browne, a fine artist as well as a writer, made his sketch in 1864. One artist, Samuel Chamberlain, was handcuffed for his trouble.

Chamberlain was with the U.S. Dragoons who passed through in 1848. He would become known for his book, *My Confessions*, and his drawings of battles and Army life during the war with Mexico. Like fellow traveler Lieutenant Couts, he was taken with San Xavier. Their commanding officer was a man fond of drink but not, it would seem, of art. Catching Chamberlain sketching the mission, he ordered him tied up and handcuffed. The next day, Chamberlain was at it again, sketching Tucson. And, again, he was punished. He deserted, joining a particularly

(ABOVE) *The face of Jesus suffering on the cross is among the most expressive images in Mission San Xavier. Photographer Richard Maack chose to focus on the face and shot upward.*
(RIGHT) *Photographers constantly search for the ideal angle and light as they take pictures of the straight and curved forms that make up Mission San Xavier. The redness in this photograph by Randy Prentice emanates from a setting sun. The cross at right binds the expansive scene into a cohesive one.*

unsavory band of scalp hunters led by John Glanton, and went on to more adventures recounted in his book. For the record, his sketch of San Xavier is the oldest known surviving drawing of the mission.

Artists and their pads and easels remain part of the San Xavier landscape, but it is the photographers who abound. The church is said to be the second most photographed subject in Arizona, the honor of first place going to the Grand Canyon. The elegant little church in the middle of a stark setting is a beguiling subject for the professional "shooters," including those of highest rank. Ansel Adams photographed the mission for the April 1954 issue of *Arizona Highways* in both color and his trademark black and white.

Amateur photographers have

(ABOVE) Burning votive candles are an eternal fixture at the feet of a statue of St. Joseph in the west transept. Jack Dykinga took the photograph before the latest preservation effort.
(OPPOSITE PAGE) Ansel Adams, especially noted for his work in black and white photography, chose to use color for this image he called Ecce Homo, *the Suffering Savior. Sunlight filtering through windows in San Xavier's great dome accentuates the image's somberness.*

always traded shot for shot with the professionals at the mission. San Xavier was as much a subject for the cameras 100 years ago as it is today. Pictures are snapped for friends, families, photo albums, and, at times, as one of the first steps in a new career.

Professional photographer Don Stevenson first visited the mission in 1971. "And everything I did was wrong. The light was wrong, the time of day was wrong, the angle was wrong, I didn't have the right lens." The picture, he reports, turned out "horribly." Then he adds, "But I fell in love with the place."

John Schaefer had also gone out to the mission over the years, taking snapshots, "the way every other tourist does," he remembers. But in the 1970s, when he was president of the University of Arizona, the mission became the subject of his first photographic project, one suggested to him by Ansel Adams. Schaefer's work would appear in the book *Bac*, written by San Xavier Fathers Celestine Chinn and Kieran McCarty. Schaefer photographed at the mission for months.

"The statues became people, and they were very forgiving because if I fouled up on exposure or the lighting, I could come back the next day or any other time and redo it until I got it right." He was dealing

JACK DYKINGA

with one of the problems presented by the interior of the church, the lack of light. While the afternoon sun from one of the high windows may gilt the angels within the chapel of the Sorrowing Mother, the photographer needs more than one moving sun beam.

States Jack Dykinga, who has photographed the mission countless times, "The inside is more of a technical problem. It's

kind of surmounted when you bring lights and ladders into play." His work with the interior in 1997 required hours of setting up special lighting before any actual photography could begin.

It was the same when Don Stevenson recorded the preservation efforts of the mid-1990s. He needed to compensate for the combination of low natural light and fluorescent lighting,

ECCE HOMO - THE SUFFERING SAVIOR, 1954 PHOTOGRAPH BY ANSEL ADAMS.

as well as for the movement of the conservators at work. For the former he used a time exposure, for the latter, time exposure plus a strobe.

Decades earlier, Schaefer, shooting in black and white, worked with available light. "A 15-minute exposure was no problem for me," he recalls.

Photographers of the late 19th century dealt with the light levels in much the same way. The shock-still portrait subjects of the period attest to the use of long time exposure. At San Xavier, they could also add a high burst of light with flash powder. What they didn't have to deal with was another challenge contemporary photographers face — people.

People and the trappings of the modern world can confound the photographer in search of an image of the timeless beauty of San Xavier. In 1997, photographers Richard Maack and Jack Dykinga worked at capturing the "grand view" of the interior. They worked alone late into the night. Maack was surprised at what he saw. "The way the restoration glowed, the silver leaf and the gold leaf, the way it reflected the light."

A few weeks later he worked in the interior during the daylight hours. What surprised him then, he reports, were "the crowds."

Another photographer, Randy Prentice, describes his view of the mission as "an array of angles, shapes, patterns, shadows." He also sees "the telephone poles, the cars, the human element."

That element has sent professional photographers scrambling for uncluttered shots. Esther Henderson was climbing the hills 50 years ago in search of one. Henderson, who was among *Arizona Highways'* first photographers, began her professional career in Tucson during the 1930s. She found her perfect angle of San Xavier on the hill of the cross. She put the cross and the mission in the foreground of the picture while blocking the parking lot with the cross' stone base.

Fifty years later, she recalled, "That was a good result because it accentuated the cross, which, I felt, was the essence of the mission, all missions for that matter."

The picture also was taken early in the morning. The light at that time of day can compel the photographer. But, so can the absence of all but the most faithful visitors.

"That's the ideal time to shoot the exterior for me," says Stevenson. "And it's quiet and the doves are singing. Nobody's up and around yet."

Others choose the early evening. "I go out late in the last half of the day," says Prentice, who also finds his window of photographic opportunity in the short days of December.

"And you can actually get the last light of the day shining on the front of it. Mainly because the sun is so far to the south."

For Schaefer, a summer day provided him with one of his favorite pictures, taken of the dome through the arches.

"I waited until the summer solstice to get the sun just right, to get the light on the dome, the cross against the sky … timing is important." But not everything. There is also

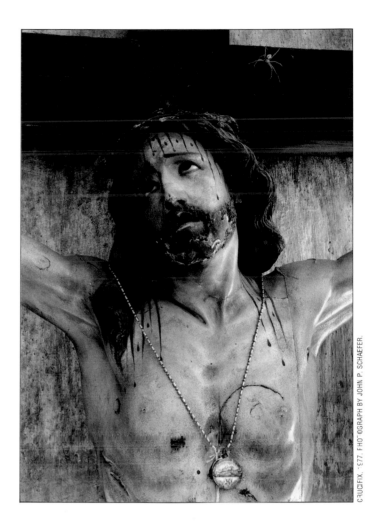

CRUCIFIX, *C77. PHOTOGRAPH BY JOHN P. SCHAEFER.*

(ABOVE) *This photograph of the suffering Christ shows how shooting the same statue from a different camera angle can subtly alter the figure's expression. Compare this view with the photograph on page 68.*

(OPPOSITE PAGE) *Shadows at sunrise accentuate the mission's white walls and dome, as seen through the north court's arches.*

DON STEVENSON

it fenced with walls and without, before the earthquake, and amidst its rubble.

The interior has been captured in the darkness of the old photography, with the blurring of the paintings and decorations by time and humanity, and in the light that came with the cleaning.

Still, with all the images that have gone before, this relatively small subject continues to beguile and challenge those who see it through a lens.

Henderson wrote of her work at San Xavier a half a century ago, "I was always in a state of despair, not happiness, feeling that no matter what I did, I could never do justice to it. I feel this way about all great places."

Says Stevenson, "To me it's all in the same category as the Grand Canyon and the red rocks of Sedona, just because of its beauty."

For those who would capture that beauty on film, he recommends using a tripod and long exposure for work in the interior. "And we are probably looking at one, two, three, four seconds of exposure at least."

There is also time to be taken in studying the subject. "We just don't snap the face of it anymore," he says. "We walk it, walk it, and rewalk it. And we watch it at different times of the day."

"It's like any of the great icons," states Dykinga, "the photographic touchstones that

(ABOVE) *For photographer Don Stevenson, the sunlight filtering into the interior through the high, small windows presents its own challenge and the need for man-made illumination.*
(RIGHT) *Richard Maack chose an angle tying together several elements of Mission San Xavier — the retablo mayor, the scalloped pews in the nave, the two angels stationed at the transept entrances, and the arches supporting the domes.*

location, location, location, and how to find it.

There is a bit of tongue-in-cheek advice given to those in search of a good picture. Stand in the footprints of the good photographers, it goes, and put the legs of your tripod down in three holes left by theirs. The problem at San Xavier is that the land is all but cratered with the footprints of the greats, the church interior all but pockmarked with the tripod holes of the gifted.

"To get something that's brand new?" muses Willard Clay, a photographer who has worked with the exterior. "That would be difficult." One of his favorite shots was taken through the arches from the north. "Not original," he says. "Ansel Adams did the same thing."

And so did others with varying results. The mission complex has been photographed up and down, from front, back, and side, north, south, aisle to altar. The historic album shows

RICHARD MAACK

people have gone to before. Each time you go there, you learn something new about the light, because each time it's changing."

Commenting on his own experience at the mission, Schaefer says, "Your vision turns from just looking at it to seeing it and understanding what the architects were trying to accomplish, what the people who have made use of the mission over the centuries have done."

"I hope they preserve it forever," says Prentice. He did his part, photographing the mission the night the stars fell and the bells rang on an old church's birthday.

The Golden Hour

DOG, TRIPODS, CAMERAS AND SAN XAVIER, AZ, 1991.
PHOTOGRAPH BY DICK ARENTZ

This perspective embraces some of the work of fine-art photographer Dick Arentz, who considers San Xavier as one of the world's dozen or so photographic icons. His works are held by such institutions as the Museum of Modern Art, the National Museum of American Art, and the Corcoran Gallery.

When he was conducting a photographic seminar at San Xavier in 1991, he captured a whimsical view (above) when his students stepped away from their cameras. Before he could shoot, a dog wandered into the scene, and Arentz, believing that photography should capture the total environment, took the shot nonetheless.

His classic image of San Xavier (right), taken in 1987 with a 12-by-20-inch camera, reflects the golden hour, a time when the light is just right for photographers to convey their message. For this image, moments defined the precise time. As Arentz took one shot, the sun no longer was blocked by the wall and glared into his camera. He quickly set up six inches to the left and captured the image with the masked sun creating a halo over the structures.

SAN XAVIER DEL BAC, 1997. PHOTOGRAPH BY DICK ARENTZ.

The Golden Hour

RICHARD MAACK

As the sun sets, the brown-robed priest shoos the last of the visitors out of the church of San Xavier del Bac. The time has come to close the doors. Outside, a few people climb the hill of the cross. Others are walking to the school for a fish fry. A sign announcing it has been posted on the wall of the mission.

South in Mexico, the people of the mission chain are starting their evening in homes near the old churches. This is the land where Kino rode, where Franciscan fathers built the walls of their churches high.

Tomorrow it begins again, with the dawn and the faithful and the tourists and buses and RVs as big as hotel suites and the clicking of a thousand cameras. But now, the church is at peace, enfolded in the last of the light that does have a way of touching that west tower.

Before leaving the church, one visitor speaks to the priest, only a few words but they are enough. In a voice gentle as the night that waits beyond the doors, she says, "Thank you so much."

XAVIER GALLEGOS/TUCSON CITIZEN

(ABOVE) Winged angels are stationed on each side of the sanctuary at the entrance to each transept.
(LEFT) San Xavier parishioner Frances Martinez lights a candle.
(RIGHT) San Xavier del Bac enters its third century as a breathtaking example of what faith can conceive and what the faithful can create.
(FOLLOWING PAGE) Although tourists sometimes consider San Xavier a museum, the solemnity of the church stands out after they have left and just a piece of the sun remains above the horizon.

80